Giant Pandas: Gifts from China

By Allan Fowler

Consultants

Robert L. Hillerich, Professor Emeritus,
Bowling Green State University, Bowling Green, Ohio;
Consultant, Pinellas County Schools, Florida

Lynne Kepler, Educational Consultant

Fay Robinson, Child Development Specialist

CHILDRENS PRESS®
CHICAGO

Design by Herman Adler Design Group
Photo Research by Feldman & Associates, Inc.

Library of Congress Cataloging-in-Publication Data

Fowler, Allan.
  Giant pandas: gifts from China / by Allan Fowler.
    p. cm. – (Rookie read-about science)
    ISBN 0-516-06031-7
    1. Giant panda—Juvenile literature. [1. Giant panda. 2. Pandas.]
  I. Title. II. Series.
QL737.C214F69   1995
599.74'443–dc20   94-38025
                                                              CIP
                                                               AC

People everywhere love pandas. Yet most people have never seen a panda — except in photos or on TV.

Giant pandas are among the rarest animals.

At the time this book is being written, there are only two giant pandas in the entire United States.

They are "star" attractions at the National Zoo in Washington, D.C.

And just a few other zoos in the world have giant pandas.

The pandas were given to those zoos as an act of friendship by the government of China.

China is the only country
where giant pandas live
in the wild.

A giant panda has a white face with black ears, a black nose, and black patches around the eyes.

Its body is white, except for black legs and a black band across its shoulders.

You can tell from a panda's thick fur that its home forests are very cold.

The part of China where
pandas make their home
has many mountains covered
with forests of bamboo.

Bamboo is a panda's favorite food.

Though it looks like a tree, bamboo is really a grass with tall, hollow stalks.

Zoos make sure that their pandas get plenty of bamboo to eat, along with fruits, vegetables, and other foods.

Pandas spend much of
their time eating.

They eat sitting up or lying on their backs. They use their paws to strip the leaves from bamboo stalks.

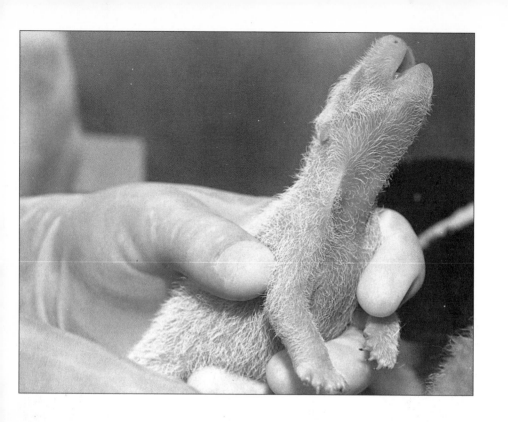

A newborn panda cub is
tiny. At first, its pink skin
shows through the fine
white fur.

In a few weeks, it has the black-and-white markings of its mother. A panda cub loves to play.

When this cub grows up, it will weigh between 200 and 300 pounds, more than most adult people.

Giant pandas look like bears, and sometimes they are called "panda bears."

But they aren't bears.

Some zoologists — scientists who study animals — think pandas might be related to raccoons.

Besides giant pandas, there is a much smaller animal called a lesser panda.

It is reddish brown in color and looks more like a raccoon than a giant panda does.

Giant pandas are endangered animals. Not even a thousand of them are known to live in the wild.

One reason pandas are endangered is that people have cut down many of the forests where they live.

Without those bamboo forests to live in, there would be no pandas left.

But giant pandas are protected now.

The Chinese government has set aside forestlands, which will never be cut down, for those wonderful animals to live in.

It's good to know that there will always be a safe place in the world for giant pandas.

Words You Know

China

giant panda

lesser panda

cub

bamboo

Index

About the Author

Allan Fowler is a free-lance writer with a background in advertising. Born in New York, he lives in Chicago now and enjoys traveling.

Photo Credits